accent on

SOLOS

LEVEL TWO

by
william gillock

ISBN 978-1-4234-7579-8

 WILLIS MUSIC

EXCLUSIVELY DISTRIBUTED BY

 HAL•LEONARD®

Visit Hal Leonard Online at
www.halleonard.com

Contact us:
Hal Leonard
7777 West Bluemound Road
Milwaukee, WI 53213
Email: info@halleonard.com

In Europe, contact:
Hal Leonard Europe Limited
42 Wigmore Street
Marylebone, London, W1U 2RN
Email: info@halleonardeurope.com

In Australia, contact:
Hal Leonard Australia Pty. Ltd.
4 Lentara Court
Cheltenham, Victoria, 3192 Australia
Email: info@halleonard.com.au

Contents

[Certain titles were updated in 2020.]

Summertime Polka

William Gillock

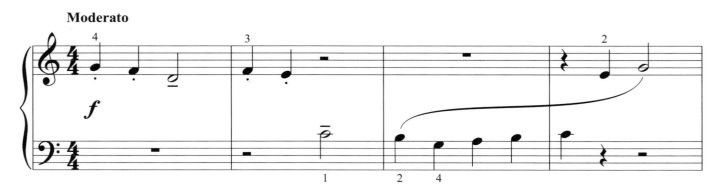

Little Gray Donkey

William Gillock

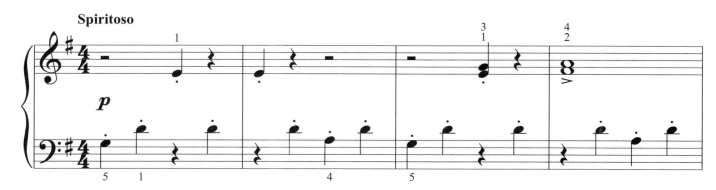

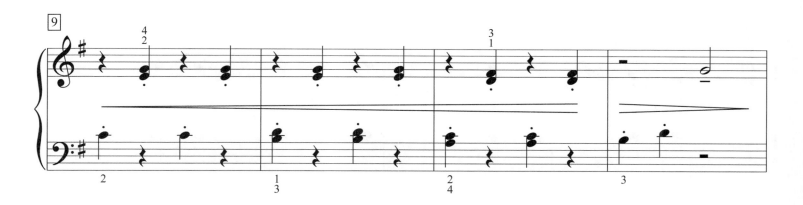

Peace Chant

William Gillock

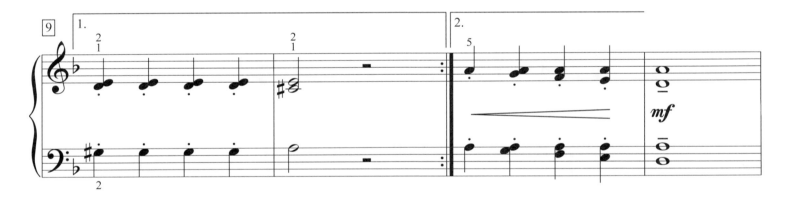

Little Flower Girl of Paris

William Gillock

Tempo di valse

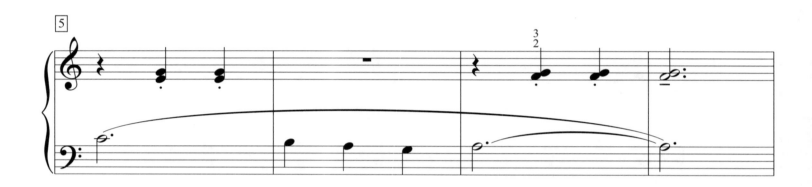

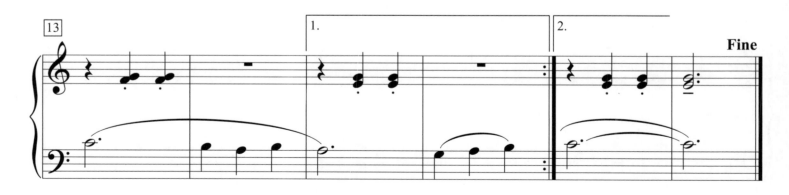

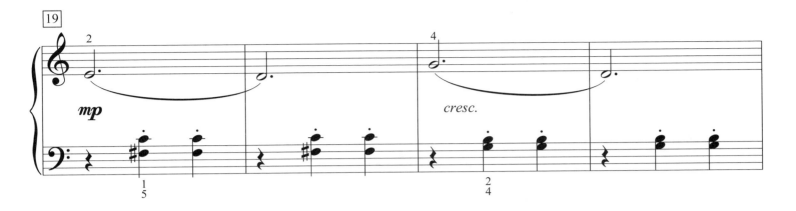

Splashing in the Brook

William Gillock

Sail Boats

William Gillock

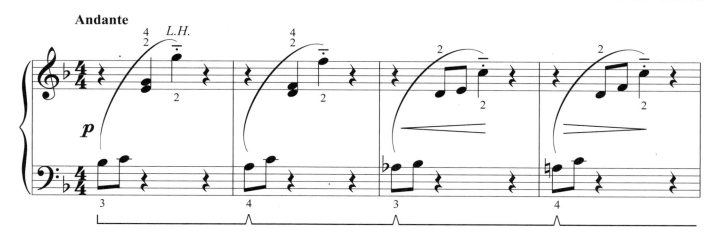

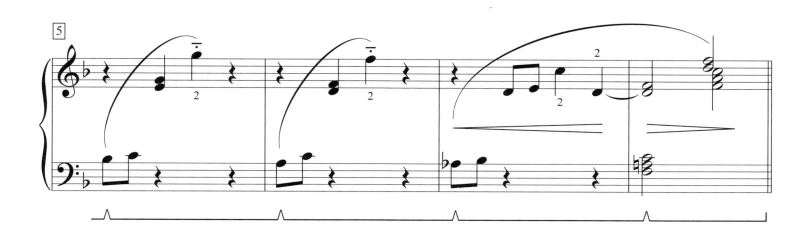

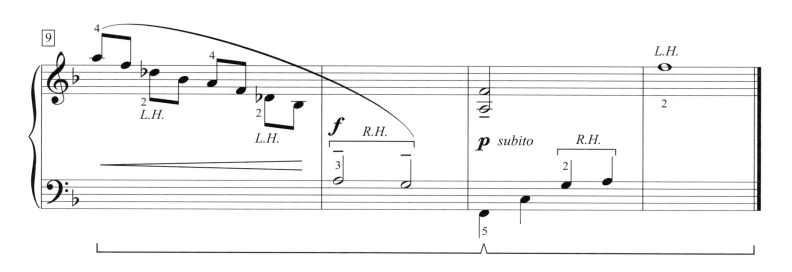

Dance Under the Stars

William Gillock

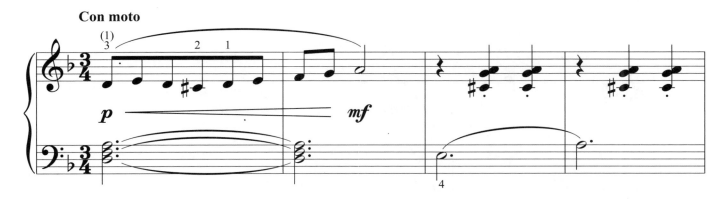

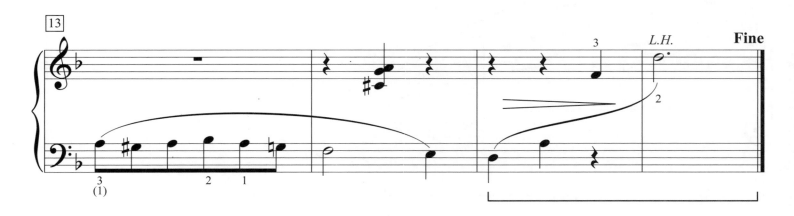

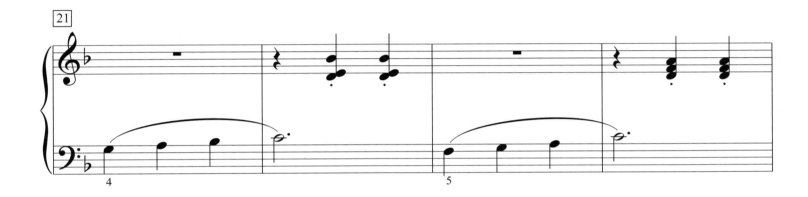

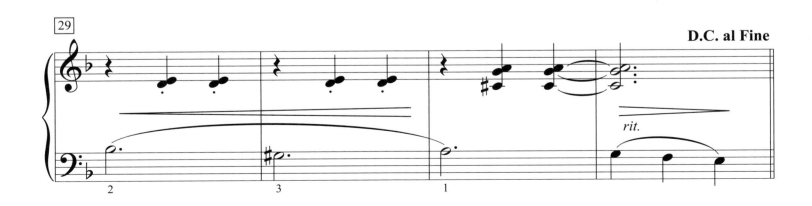

Argentina

William Gillock

Stars on a Summer Night

William Gillock

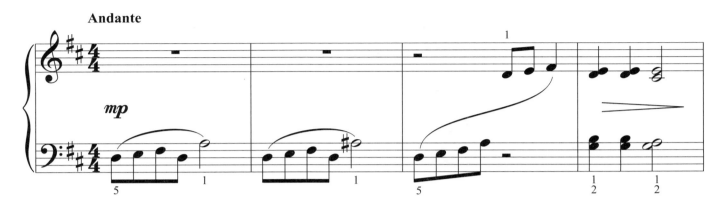

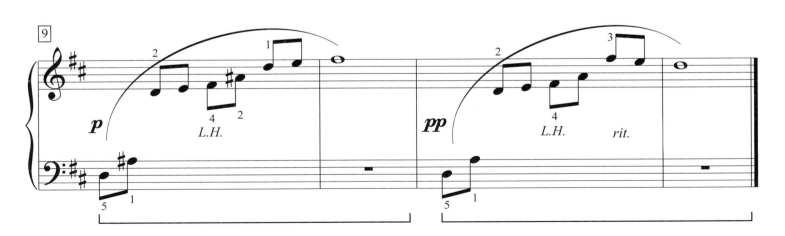

Gavotte and Musette

William Gillock

Gavotte (Lively)

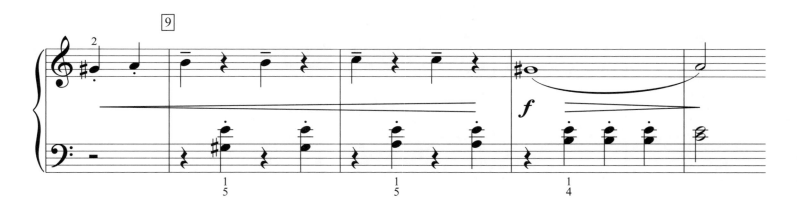

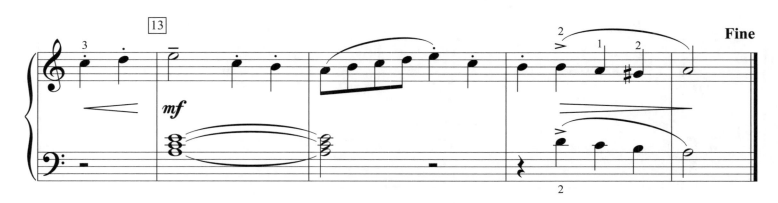

Owl at Midnight

William Gillock

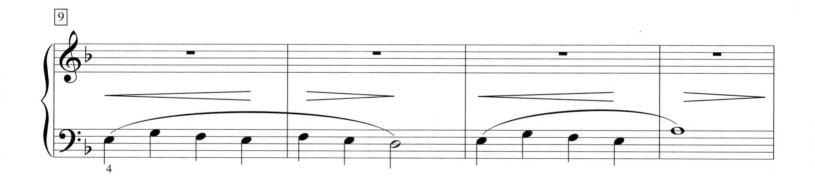

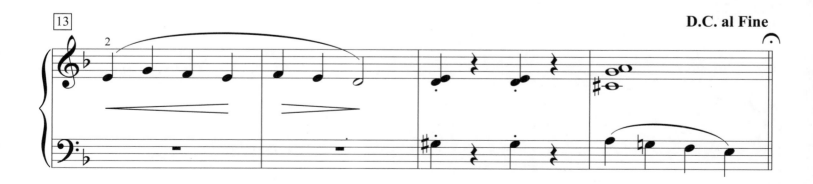